Anonymous

Everyday Cook Book

Anonymous

Everyday Cook Book

ISBN/EAN: 9783744786393

Printed in Europe, USA, Canada, Australia, Japan

Cover: Foto ©Andreas Hilbeck / pixelio.de

More available books at **www.hansebooks.com**

S. & S.
MANUAL LIBRARY.—No. 21.
ISSUED SEMI-MONTHLY.

....

SUBSCRIPTION PRICE, $2.40 PER YEAR. **FEBRUARY 1, 1891.**

Copyrighted, 1891, by Street & Smith.

Entered at the Post-Office, New York, as Second-Class Matter.

EVERYDAY

COOK BOOK.

——————

NEW YORK:
STREET & SMITH, Publishers,
31 Rose Street.

CONTENTS.

PAGE

EVERYDAY COOK BOOK.

SOUPS.

PLAIN VEAL SOUP.—Take a leg of veal and boil it with a cup two-thirds full of rice, and a pound and a half of pork; season it with salt, pepper, and sweet herbs, if you like. A little celery boiled in it gives the soup a fine flavor. The veal should be taken up before the soup is seasoned. Just before the soup is taken up, put in a couple of slices of toast, cut into small pieces.

MOCK TURTLE SOUP.—Boil a calf's head until perfectly tender; then take it out, strain the liquor, and set it away until the next day; then skim off the fat, cut up the meat, together with the lights, and put it into the liquor; put it on the fire, and season it with salt, pepper, cloves, and mace; stew it gently for half an hour. Just before you take it up, add half a pint of white wine. For the balls, chop lean veal fine, with a little salt pork; add the brains, and season it with salt, pepper, cloves, mace, and sweet herbs; make it up into balls about the size of half an egg; boil part in the soup, and fry the remainder, and put them in a dish by themselves.

BEEF SOUP.—Boil a shank of beef four or five hours in water enough to cover it. Half an hour before the soup is put on the table, take up the meat, thicken the soup with scorched flour mixed with cold water; season it with salt, pepper, cloves, and mace. A little walnut or tomato catsup improves it. Make force meat balls of part of the beef and pork, season them with mace, cloves, pepper, and salt, and boil them in the soup fifteen minutes.

CHICKEN OR TURKEY SOUP.—The liquor that a chicken or turkey is boiled in makes a good soup. Put in half a teacupful of rice, when the liquor boils, or slice up a few potatoes and put in. Season it with salt, pepper, sweet herbs, and a little celery. Toast bread or crackers, and put them in the soup when you take it up.

OYSTER SOUP.—Separate the oysters from the liquor; to each quart of the liquor put a pint of milk or water; set it on the fire with the oysters. Mix a heaping tablespoonful of flour with a little water, and stir it into the liquor as soon as it boils. Season it with salt, pepper, and a little vinegar. Put in a small lump of butter, and turn it as soon as it boils up again on to buttered toast; cut into small pieces.

PEA SOUP.—If you make your soup of dry peas, soak them over night in a warm place, using a quart of water to each quart of the peas. Early the next morning boil them an hour. Boil with them a teaspoonful of saleratus, eight or ten minutes, then take them out of the water they were soaking in, put them into fresh water, with a pound of salt pork, and boil it till the peas are soft, which will be in the course of three or four hours. Green peas for soup require no soaking, and boiling only long enough to have the pork get thoroughly cooked, which will be in the course of an hour.

PORTABLE SOUP.—Take beef or veal soup, and let it get perfectly cold, then skim off every particle of the grease. Set it on the fire, and let it boil till of a thick, glutinous consistence. Care should be taken that it does not burn. Season it highly with salt, pepper, cloves, and mace—add a little wine or brandy, and then turn it on to earthern platters. It should not be more than a quarter of an inch in thickness. Let it remain until cold, then cut it in pieces three inches square; set them in the sun to dry, turning them frequently. When perfectly dry, put them in an earthern or tin vessel, having a layer of white paper between each layer. These, if the directions are strictly attended to, will keep good a long time. Whenever you wish to make a soup of them, nothing more is necessary than to put a quart of water to one of the cakes and heat it very hot.

MACARONI SOUP.— Take a given weight of macaroni, in proportion to the quantity of soup required (say one pound), and boil it in a quart of beef or other soup, until it is tender, then take out one half and keep the other boiling until it is reduced to a pulp. Add sufficient soup until the whole, with half a pint of cream, boiling, makes five pints; grate eight ounces of Parmesan cheese, and add the half of the macaroni which had been only boiled tender, warm it without boiling, and serve with toast.

GRAVY SOUP.—Take a leg of beef, well wash and soak it, break the bone, put it into a saucepan with a gallon of water, a large bunch of sweet herbs, two large onions sliced and fried to a nice brown, taking great care they are not burnt, two blades of mace, three cloves, twenty berries of allspice, and forty of black pepper, and stew till the soup is as rich as you wish it to be, then take out the meat; when it is cold, take off the fat, heat the soup, with vermicelli, and the nicest part of a head of celery boiled and cut to pieces, cayenne, and a little salt; carrot may be added, with turnip cut up into small pieces, and boiled with spinach and endive, or the herbs without the vermicelli, or vermicelli only; add also a large spoonful of soy, and one of mushroom catsup. A French roll should be made hot and put into the soup.

Ox-Tail Soup.—Same as gravy soup, adding about three ox-tails, separated at the joints; when the meat upon them is tender, it is done; they must not be over-stewed; add a spoonful of catsup, and send to table with pieces of the tail in the soup.

Venison Soup.—Take four pounds of freshly killed venison cut off from the bones, and one pound of ham in small slices. Add an onion minced, and black pepper to your taste. Put only as much water as will cover it, and stew it gently for an hour, keeping the pot closely covered. Skim it well, and pour in a quart of boiling water. Add a head of celery cut small, and three blades of mace. Boil it gently two hours and a half; then put in quarter of a pound of butter, cut small and rolled in flour, and half-pint of Port or Madeira. Let it boil quarter of an hour longer, and send it to the table with the meat in it.

A Cheap Soup.—A pound or a pound and a half of lean beef, cut up into small pieces, six quarts of water; stew in three large onions, with double the quantity of turnips; put in thyme, parsley, pepper, and salt, half a pound of rice, a pound of potatoes peeled and cut in quarters, and a handful of oatmeal. Stew from three to four hours, not less.

MUTTON SOUP.—Cut a neck of mutton into four pieces, and put it aside, then take a slice of the gammon of bacon and put it into a saucepan with a quart of peas and enough water to boil them; let the peas boil to a pulp, then strain them through a cloth, and put them aside; add enough water to that in which is the bacon to boil the mutton; slice three turnips, as many carrots, and boil for an hour slowly, adding sweet herbs, onions, cabbage, and lettuce chopped small; then stew a quarter of an hour longer, sufficient to cook the mutton, then take it out, and take some fresh green peas, add them with some chopped parsley and the peas first boiled to the soup, put in a lump of butter rolled in flour, and stew till the green peas are done.

LAMB SOUP.—May be cooked as mutton, save that beef may be substituted for the bacon.

ESPAGNOLE.—Take fourteen pounds of the leg or shoulder of veal and an old fowl, chop the veal into pieces, and put the whole into a saucepan, with two carrots, two onions, a pound of ham, a few peppercorns, a small quantity of spice, and a clove of garlic; let this stew over the fire, shaking it frequently, till it becomes of a brown color, then add hot water to come four inches above the meat, set it by the stove to boil gently, skimming when the meat comes from the bones, strain it through a silk sieve, and set it by for use.

VEGETABLE SOUP.—Collect whatever vegetables are in season, take equal quantities, turnips, carrots, parsley, celery, leeks, six tomatoes, half cup of rice. three pounds soup meat (beef), one marrow bone. and three quarts water. Boil meat three hours, vegetables two hours.

TOMATO SOUP.—Take two pounds of soup beef, and boil in two quarts of water two hours; then add one can or one quart of tomatoes, and boil one hour longer. Just before the soup is done, add one-half teaspoonful of baking soda. Put in one quart of milk, and remove from fire soon as milk boils up.

CLAM SOUP.—Take twenty-five hard-shell clams, removed from shells. Be careful, in opening the clams, to preserve all the liquor. Place clams and liquor in two quarts of water. Boil one-half hour. Slice three potatoes thin, cut fine a little sprig of parsley. Add parsley and potatoes to the soup, and boil until potatoes are cooked. Beat one egg, add one-quarter teaspoonful of baking powder, two tablespoonfuls water, and enough flour to make soft dough. Drop dough in small spoonfuls into soup while boiling, about fifteen minutes before the whole is done. Season with salt and pepper.

RICE SOUP.—Soak four ounces of fine rice in cold water for an hour, then boil it; add three quarts of gravy. a pinch of cayenne, a little salt, and boil five minutes.

ONION SOUP.—In two quarts of weak mutton broth slice two turnips and as many carrots; then strain it. Fry six onions cut in slices; when nicely browned add them to the broth; simmer three hours, skim, and serve.

CHOWDERS.

CODFISH CHOWDER.—Fry some slices cut from the fat part of pork, in a deep stewpan, mix sliced onions with a variety of sweet herbs, and lay them on the pork; bone and cut a fresh cod into thick slices, and place them on the pork, then put a layer of slices of pork, on that a layer of hard biscuit or crackers, then alternately, the pork, fish, and crackers, with the onions and herbs scattered through them, till the pan is nearly full; season with pepper and salt; put in about two quarts of water, cover the stewpan close, and let it stand with fire above and below it four hours; then skim it well and serve it.

CLAM CHOWER.—Take half a pound of fat salt pork cut in slices, chop fine, and place in a large iron saucepan, without water; fry the pork brown, then add fifty hard-shell clams, chopped fine; also the liquor from the clams, four quarts of water, six large onions, six large potatoes, one quart of tomatoes, all chopped fine. Boil four or five hours. Add one half pound pilot biscuit, broken, and season with thyme, pepper, and salt about half an hour before done.

———

FISH.

COD FISH, BOILED.—A small fish should be selected. Tie up the head and shoulders well, place it in the kettle with enough cold water to completely cover it; cast in a handful of salt. The fish, if a small one, will be cooked in twenty

minutes after it has boiled; if large, it will take
half an hour. When done enough, drain it clear
of the scum, and remove the string; send it to
table garnished with the liver, the smelt, and the
roe of the fish, scraped horse-radish, lemon sliced,
and sprigs of parsley.

COD SCALLOPED.—Take enough cold dressed cod
to nearly fill all the shells you purpose using, pound
it, beat up the yolk of an egg and pour over it,
add a few shrimps skinned, salt, pepper, and a
little butter; do not quite fill the shells, strew
over them fine bread crumbs, and drop butter in a
liquid state over them. Brown them before the
fire in a Dutch oven.

TAIL OF A COD.—Boil as previously directed,
and when sufficiently done, divide it into moderate
sized pieces, and in a light batter fry them brown.
Send up crisped parsley with it as a garnish.

BAKED COD.—Cut a large fine piece out of the
middle of the fish, and skin it carefully; stuff it
with a stuffing composed of the yolks of two eggs
boiled hard, the roe half-boiled, bread crumbs,
grated lemon-peel. butter, pepper, and salt to
taste. Blind it with the undressed white of an
egg, and sew in the stuffing with white thread,
bake it in a Dutch oven before the fire, turn it
frequently, and baste it with butter; serve with
shrimp sauce. plain butter, or oyster sauce. A tin
baking-dish is preferable to any other for cooking
this fish.

COD-FISH PIE.—Take a piece from the middle
of a good sized fish, salt it well all night, then
wash it, and season with salt. pepper, and a few
grains of nutmeg. a little chopped parsley and
some oysters. put all in your dish, with pieces of
butter on the fish; add a cup of good second white

stock and cream; cover it with a good crust, adding a little lemon juice in the gravy.

SALT COD.—Soak the fish for eight hours in clean cold water (not spring water), let the water have enough vinegar in it to impregnate it with a slight flavor and no more after soaking the above time, take it out and let it drain three or four hours, then put in soak again for four hours; when this has been done, place it in a fish-kettle with plenty of cold soft water, let it come to a boil very slowly, place it on the side of the fire, and it will cook gradually until enough. Serve with parsnips and egg sauce.

CURRIED COD.—Cut some handsome steaks of cod, slice a number of onions, and fry both a good brown color, stew the fish in white gravy, add a large teaspoonful of curry powder, a third that quantity of cayenne pepper, thicken with three spoonfuls of cream, a little butter, a pinch of salt, and a little flour.

CRIMPED COD.—Cut the cod in slices, and lay it for about three hours in spring water salted, adding one wine-glassful of vinegar; make a fish kettle three parts full of spring water, in which a large handful of salt has been thrown, let it boil quickly, put in the cod, and keep it boiling for ten minutes; take up the slices of fish, garnish with sprigs of parsley, sliced lemon, and horse-radish scraped into curls; serve with shrimp and oyster sauce.

STEWED COD.—Cut some of the finest pieces from the thickest part of the fish, place them in a stewpan with a lump of butter the size of a walnut, or larger, three or four blades of mace, bread crumbs, pepper, salt, a small bunch of sweet herbs, and some oysters, with a little of their own liquor. When nearly done, add a large wine-glass of sherry, and stew gently until enough.

FRESH HERRINGS BAKED.—Wash the herrings in clear spring water, and when they are thoroughly clean, drain them, and then, without wiping them, lay them in a dish or baking-pan; pepper and salt them, chop finely two or three onions, some parsley, thyme, and strew over them; cover them in equal proportions of vinegar and small beer; tie them over, and let them bake one hour in a slow oven. They should be kept in the pickle, and make a pleasant dish when cold.

FRESH HERRINGS BOILED.—Clean them, wash them over with vinegar, and put them in boiling water; they will take from ten to twelve minutes. Garnish with parsley, and serve melted butter, in which a tablespoonful of catsup, a teaspoonful of Chili vinegar, and one of made mustard has been mixed while making.

FRESH HERRINGS BROILED.—Steep them first in vinegar and water into which a handful of salt has been thrown; let them remain ten minutes, then take them out and broil them over a clear fire. Serve. garnished with parsley. They may be eaten with melted butter, with a little mustard and vinegar in it, or lemon juice instead of the latter, being preferable.

FRESH HERRINGS FRIED.—Slice small onions, and lay in the pan with the fish, or fry separately. Serve the fish with the onions laid round them. The herrings are generally fried without the onions, but those who are partial to this strongly-flavored vegetable will prefer the addition.

TO POT HERRINGS.—Take from one to two dozen herrings, according to the number you purpose potting. Take two ounces of salt, one of saltpeter, two of allspice, reduce them to an impalpable powder, and rub them well into the herrings; let them remain with the spice upon them eight hours to drain, wipe off the spice clean, and lay them on a pan on which butter has been rubbed; season with nutmeg, mace, pepper, salt, and one clove, in powder, one ounce each, save the last; lay in two or three bay leaves, cover with butter, and bake gently three hours. When cool, drain off the liquor, pack the fish in the pots intended for their use, cover to the depth of half an inch with clarified butter, sufficiently melted just to run, but do not permit it to be hot; they will be ready for eating in two days.

LOBSTER CURRIED.—Take the meat of a fine lobster, or two, if small, place in a stewpan two dessert-spoonfuls of curry powder, add two ounces of butter, an onion cut in very fine strips, and three dessert-spoonfuls of fish stock. When they are stewed well, add the lobster, simmer gently an hour, squeeze in half a lemon, and season with a little salt.

LOBSTER STEWED.—Extract from the shells of two lobsters, previously boiled, all of the meat; take two-thirds of a quart of water, and stew the shells in it, with mace, unground pepper, and salt. Let it boil an hour or more, till you have obtained all that is to be gotten from them; then strain. Add the richest portions of the lobster, and some of the best of the firm meat, to some thin melted butter; squeeze a little lemon juice into it, add a tablespoonful of Madeira, pour this into the gravy, and, when warmed, it is ready to serve.

LOBSTER BUTTER.—The hen lobster should be selected, on account of the corals; take out the

meat and spawn, and bruise it in a mortar; add to
it a teaspoonful of white wine, season with pepper,
salt, nutmeg, and a little grated lemon peel; add
four ounces of butter, slightly dusted over with
flour. Work this well together, and rub it through
a hair sieve. It should be kept in a cool place till
ready to serve.

To ROAST LOBSTERS.—Take a live lobster, half
boil it, take it from the kettle in which it is boiling, dry it with a cloth, and while hot, rub it over
with butter, and set it before a good fire, basting
it with butter; when it produces a fine froth, it is
done. Serve with melted butter.

To BOIL MACKEREL.—Clean the fish thoroughly,
remove the roe, steep it in vinegar and water, and
replace it; place the fish in water from which the
chill has been taken, and boil very slowly from
fifteen to twenty minutes; garnish with parsley,
and chopped parsley in melted butter; serve up as
sauce.

To BAKE MACKEREL.—Open and clean thoroughly, wipe very dry, pepper and salt the inside,
and put in a stuffing composed of powdered bread
crumbs, the roe chopped small, parsley, and sweet
herbs, but very few of the latter, work these
together with the yolk of an egg, pepper and salt
to taste, and sew it in the fish; then place the
latter in a deep baking dish, and dredge it with
flour, slightly, adding a little cold butter in small
pieces; put the fish into an oven, and twenty-eight
or thirty minutes will suffice to cook them. Send
them in a hot dish to table, with parsley and
butter.

To BROIL MACKEREL.—Cleanse it well, and cut
with a sharp knife a gash from head to tail, just
sufficient on one side to clear the backbone, pass

into the incision a little pepper (cayenne) and salt, moistened with clarified butter, broil it over a clear fire; the sides being the thinnest part, they will be first done; therefore, when they are done, take the fish off the gridiron, and hold it in front of the fire for five minutes, the back of the fish being next the fire, and the fish will be thoroughly done; this is the readiest and most effective mode. The sauce may be the same as for boiled mackerel, or sauce a la maitre d'hotel.

TO FRY MACKEREL. — Thoroughly clean the fish, cut off the tails, and with a sharp knife lay the fish completely open, and remove the backbone. Dry the mackerel thoroughly, sprinkle with powdered salt and pepper, dredge with flour, and, when the lard in the frying-pan is boiling, lay them in, and fry them a clear brown.

ROAST OYSTERS.—Large oysters not opened; a few minutes before they are wanted, put them on a gridiron over a moderate fire. When done they will open. Do not lose the liquor that is in the shell with the oysters. Serve them hot upon a napkin.

AN OYSTER PIE, WITH SWEETBREADS.—Blanch them, and take off the beards; separate them from the liquor, blanch some throat sweetbreads, and when cold, cut them in slices, then lay them and the oysters in layers in your dish, and season with salt, pepper, and a few grains of mace and nutmeg; add some thick sauce, a little cream, and the oyster liquor, and some good veal stock; bake in a slow oven.

STEWED OYSTERS.—The oysters should be bearded and rinsed in their own liquor, which should then be strained and thickened with flour and butter and placed with the oysters in a stewpan; add mace, lemon peel cut into shreds, and some white pepper whole; these ingredients had better be confined in a piece of muslin. The stew must simmer only—if it is suffered to boil, the oysters will become hard; serve with sippets of bread. This may be varied by adding a glass of wine to the liquor, before the oysters are put in and warmed.

SCALLOPED OYSTERS.—Beard the oysters, wash in their own liquor, steep bread crumbs in the latter. put them with the oysters into scallop shells, with a bit of butter, and seasoning of salt, pepper, and a little grated nutmeg; make a paste with bread crumbs and butter; cover, and roast them before the fire, or in an oven.

OYSTER FRITTERS.—Beard, dip them into an omelet, sprinkle well with crumbs of bread, and fry them brown.

TO BAKE PIKE.—Clean and empty the fish thoroughly, stuff it with oyster forcemeat. sprinkle over it a little salt, and dredge a little flour, stick small pieces of butter over it, and bake in a steady oven forty to fifty minutes; this must be regulated by the size of the fish. To the sauce which will be found in the dish when the pike is done, a little melted butter with a spoonful of essence of anchovies may be added, and a small quantity of grated lemon peel or lemon pickle.

TO BOIL PIKE.—Having cleaned well, lay it upon a drainer and put it in the fish kettle. let it have plenty of water, into which you may throw a handful of salt and a glassful of vinegar; when it boils, remove the scum as fast as it rises; it will take three quarters of an hour dressing, if a tolerable size; if very large, an hour; if small, half an hour; serve with melted butter and lemon sliced or whole.

To BROIL SHAD.—Clean, wash, and split the shad, wipe it dry and sprinkle it with pepper and salt; broil it like mackerel.

To FRY SHAD.—Clean the fish, cut off the head, and split it down the back; save the roe and eggs when taking out the entrails. Cut the fish in pieces about three inches wide, rinse each in cold water, and dry on a cloth; use wheat flour to rub each piece. Have ready hot salted lard and lay in the fish, inside down, and fry till of a fine brown, then turn and fry the other side. Fry the roe and eggs with the fish.

To BAKE A SHAD, ROCK-FISH, OR BASS.—Clean the fish carefully, sprinkle it lightly with salt and let it lie a few minutes; then wash it, season it slightly with cayenne pepper and salt, and fry it gently a light brown. Prepare a seasoning of bread crumbs, pounded mace and cloves, majoram, parsley, cayenne pepper, and salt; strew it over and in the fish; let it stand an hour. Put it in a deep dish, and set it in the oven to bake; to a large fish, put in the dish half pint of water, one pint of wine, Port and Madeira mixed, half teacupful of mushrooms or tomato catsup; to a small one allow in proportion the same ingredients; baste frequently, and garnish with sliced lemon.

CRABS—To DRESS CRABS.—Scoop the meat from the shell mix the meat into a paste with a little vinegar, bread crumbs. grated nutmeg. and a little butter, or sweet oil; return it into the shell, and serve. To serve this hot. it should be heated before the fire, and served up with dry toast cut into large squares or dice.

BAKED CRABS.—Remove the meat from the shell, mix it with bread crumbs—about one-fourth will be sufficient; add white pepper, salt, a little cayenne, grated nutmeg, and half a dozen small lumps of butter, each about the size of a nut; this last ingredient should be added to the fish after it had been returned to the shell. Squeeze lemon juice over it; lay a thick coat of bread crumbs over all, and bake.

EELS BREAD-CRUMBED.—Cut your fish into two-inch pieces, dry and flour them, and proceed as for other fried fish, dishing them on a napkin with fried parsley.

FRIED EELS.—Cut into pieces same length as above, cleaned nicely and well- dried; let them be coated with yolk of egg, powdered with bread-crumbs; fry them brown; serve with parsley and butter, and garnish with handsome sprigs of parsley.

BOILED EELS.—Choose the smallest, simmer in a small quantity of water, into which a quantity of parsley has been put. Garnish and serve with same sauce as the last.

EELS STEWED.—To stew eels, they should be cut in pieces about three inches long, and fried until they are about half cooked; they will be then brown; let them get cold, take some good beef gravy, and an onion, parsley, plenty of white pepper, a little salt. some sage chopped very fine, enough only to add to the flavor, and a little mace, place the eels in this gravy, and stew until they are tender; two anchovies may be finely chopped and added, with two teaspoonfuls of mustard, already made, some walnut catsup, and a glass of red wine; serve with sippets of toasted bread.

Or, after being stewed until tender, a glass of port wine may be added, half a lemon squeezed into it; strain, and thicken with butter and flour.

HALIBUT STEWED.—Put in a stewpan half a pint of fish broth, a tablespoonful of vinegar, and one of mushroom catsup; add an anchovy, two good-sized onions cut in quarters, a bunch of sweet herbs, and one clove of garlic; also add a pint and a half of water, and let it stew an hour and a quarter; then strain it off clear, and put into it the head and shoulders of a fine halibut and stew until tender; thicken with butter and flour, and serve.

HALIBUT COLLOPED.—Cut the fish into nice cutlets, of about an inch thick, and fry them; then put them into a broth made of the bones, four onions, a stick of celery, and a bundle of sweet herbs, boiled together for one half an hour.

TO BOIL HALIBUT.—Take a halibut, or what you require. Put it into the fish-kettle with the back of the fish undermost, cover it with cold water, in which a handful of salt, and a bit of saltpeter the size of a hazel nut, have been dissolved. When it begins to boil, skim it carefully, and then let it just simmer till it is done. Four pounds of fish will require nearly thirty minutes, to boil it. Drain it, garnish with horse-radish— egg sauce or plain melted butter is served with it.

TO BOIL SALMON.—This fish cannot be cooked too soon after being caught; it should be put into a kettle with plenty of cold water and a handful of salt; the addition of a small quantity of vinegar will add to the firmness of the fish; let it boil gently. For four pounds of salmon, fifty minutes will be enough; if thick, a few minutes more may be allowed. Garnish with parsley.

SALMON BROILED.—Cut the fish in inch slices from the best part, season well with pepper and salt; wrap each slice in white paper, which has been buttered with fresh butter; fasten each end by twisting or tying; broil over a very clear fire eight minutes. A coke fire, if kept clear and bright, is best. Serve with butter, anchovy, or tomato sauce.

DRIED SALMON BROILED.—Cut and cook as above, save that when it is warmed through it is enough. Serve plain, if for breakfast, or with egg sauce, if for dinner.

SALMON ROASTED.—Take a large piece of the middle of a very fine salmon, dredge well with flour, and while roasting baste it with butter. Serve, garnished with lemon.

STEWED SALMON.—Scrape the scales clean off, cut it in slices, stew them in rich white gravy; add, immediately previous to serving. one table-spoonful of essence of anchovies, a little parsley, chopped very fine, and a pinch of salt.

SALMON POTTED.—Cut a handsome piece from the middle of the salmon; remove the scales, and wipe it with a clean cloth. Rub into it some common salt thoroughly. Beat up some mace, cloves, and whole pepper, and season the salmon with it; place it in a pan with a few bay leaves; cover it with butter. and bake it until thoroughly done; remove it from the gravy, letting it drain thoroughly, then place it in the pots. Clarify sufficient butter to cover all the pots after the salmon has been put into them; put it to cool.

TO PICKLE SALMON.—Scale. clean, split, and divide the salmon into handsome pieces; place them in the bottom of a stewpan, with just suffi-

cient water to cover them. Put into three quarts
of water one pint of vinegar, a dozen bay leaves,
half that quantity of mace, a handful of salt, and
a fourth part of an ounce of black pepper. When
the salmon is sufficiently boiled remove it, drain
it, and place it upon a cloth. Put in the kettle
another layer of salmon, pour cver it the liquor
which you have prepared, and keep it until the
salmon is done. Then remove the fish, place it in
a deep dish or pan, and cover it with the pickle,
which, if not sufficiently acid. mav receive more
vinegar and salt, and be boiled forty minutes.
Let the air be kept from the fish, and, if kept for
any length of time, it will be found necessary to
occasionally drain the liquor from the fish, and
skim, and boil it.

QUENELLES OR PUDDING.—Use any salmon you
may have left, pick it free from all bones and skin,
put crumbs of a French roll, or some light
crums of bread, in a half-pint of milk, a sprig of
parsley, a small shallot. or onion, put it all to boil
until dried up, stir, it and keep it from burning,
then put it to get cold; pound the salmon well,
then add boiled fat, take out the onion and
parsley, and put about two ounces of butter with
it; pound all well, then rub it through a wire sieve;
when done, return it back into the mortar, and
add, according to the quantity, two yolks of eggs
and one whole egg, a little essence of anchovies,
cayenne pepper. salt, and a dust of sugar. Have
a stewpan of boiling water ready; take out a piece
and boil it to see if it is light, or does not drop to
pieces; have your small or large molds ready, and
well buttered; six small ones are sufficient for a
dish; if for a corner put buttered paper over each
mold. To stew them, have a stewpan large
enough to hold them, line the bottom with paper,

and only put sufficient water to be half up the mold; mind the cover fits close, and be sure it boils, then put them in; the small ones will take about half an hour; when done drain the grease well from them, before dishing; pour the sauce in the middle.

TROUT.—Scale, gut, clean, dry, and flour, then fry them in butter until they are rich clear brown; fry some green parsley crisp, and make some plain melted butter, put in one teaspoonful of essence of anchovy, and one glass of white wine; garnish, when the trouts are dished, with the crisp parsley and lemon cut in slices; the butter may be poured over the fish, but it is most advisable to send it in a butter tureen.

TROUT STEWED.—First wash and clean the fish, wipe it perfectly dry, put into a stewpan two ounces of butter, dredge in flour as it melts, and add grated nutmeg, a little mace, and a little cayenne. Stew well, and when fluid and thoroughly mixed, lay in the fish, which having suffered to slightly brown, cover with a pint of veal gravy; throw in a little salt, a small faggot of parsley, and a few rings of lemon peel; stew slowly forty minutes, then take out the fish, strain the gravy clear, and pour it over the fish.

To BOIL PERCH.—First wipe or wash off the slime, then scrape off the scales, which adhere rather tenaciously to this fish; empty and clean the insides perfectly, take out the gills, cut off the fins, and lay the perch into equal parts of cold and of boiling water, salted as for mackerel. From eight to ten minutes will boil them unless they are very large. Dish them on a napkin, garnish them with curled parsley, and serve melted butter with them.

CRAB SALAD.—Extract the fish from the shell, and place in the center of the dish in which it is to be served, in the form of a pyramid; arrange the salad round tastefully and add salad mixture. This dish is not infrequently garnished with the smallest claws of the fish.

MEATS.

ROASTING.—In every case where meat is washed before roasting, it should be well dried before it is put down to the fire, which must be kept clear, banked up to the height it is intended to keep it, and kept at that height until the meat is sufficiently cooked. Remember the regulation of gradually advancing the meat nearer the fire while it is cooking; baste with a little milk and water, or salt and water first, but as soon as the fat begins to fall from the meat, put down a clean dish, and then baste with the dripping as it falls; the meat should not be sprinkled with salt until nearly cooked, or too much gravy will be produced.

TO ROAST BEEF.—The primest parts are roasted, except the round, which should be boiled; the ribs make the finest roasting joint. Where a small quantity is required, it is better for the bones to be cut out, and the meat rolled; this should be done by the butcher. In roasting the ribs, or any piece of beef, precautions mentioned respecting placing it too near the fire must be observed; and where there is much fat, and it is desired to preserve it from being cooked before the lean, it may be covered with clean white paper skewered over it; when it is nearly done the paper should be removed, a little flour dredged over it, and a rich frothy appearance will be obtained. The joint should be served up with potatoes and other vegetables: the dish should be garnished around the edge with horse-radish scraped into thin curls. This receipt will suffice for all the other roasting parts of beef.

To Cook the Inside of the Sirloin.—Take out the inside of the sirloin in one piece, put it into a stewpan, with sufficient good gravy to cover it; season with mixed spice, pepper, salt, and cayenne, and a spoonful of walnut catsup; more of the latter may be added, if the quantity made should require it to flavor; serve with pickled gherkins cut small.

Fillet of Beef Roasted.—The fillet, which comes from the inside of the sirloin, may be larded or roasted plain; for high dinners it is larded. Baste with fresh butter. It must be a large fillet which takes longer than an hour and twenty minutes; serve with tomato sauce, and garnish with horse-radish, unless served with currant jelly, then serve as with venison or hare.

Rump Steak Stewed.—Cut a steak about an inch thick, with a good bit of fat, fry it over a brisk fire, place it in a stewpan with the gravy, a little good stock, a little port wine, and some chopped mushrooms, and stew gently; when tender, put into the stewpan some good brown sauce; shake it gently about; then dish it, and put scraped or grated horse-radish on the top; if for oysters or mushrooms, season plentifully with salt, cayenne pepper, and sugar.

Rump Steak Broiled.—Cut your steak not so thick as for the former; have ready a good, clear fire, and get your gridiron quite hot: then put on the steak at full length, frequently stirring it with your steak tongs; a few minutes, according to taste, will do it; place it on your dish, rub a good slice of butter all over it, and now pepper and salt it. Serve with a horse-radish on the top of it, and, frequently, sauces.

BEEF STEAKS BROILED.—Be particular that the fire is clear; when the meat is browned, turn it; do not be afraid of doing this often, as this is the best plan to preserve the gravy. When they are done, rub them over with a piece of fresh butter, pepper, and salt them, sprinkle the shallot, or onion cut very small, and send them to table with oyster sauce, a dish of nicely-cooked greens, and well-boiled potatoes.

BEEF KIDNEYS—STEWED.—Procure a couple of very fine beef kidneys, cut them in slices, and lay them in a stewpan; put in two ounces of butter, and four large onions cut into very thin slices: add to them a sufficiency of pepper and salt to season well. Stew them about an hour; add a cupful of rich gravy to that extracted from the kidney. Stew five minutes, strain it, and thicken the gravy with flour and butter, give it a boil up. Serve with the gravy in the dish.

BEEF HEART ROASTED.—Wash thoroughly, stuff with forcemeat, send it to table as hot as it is possible with currant jelly sauce; it will take about forty minutes' roasting.

BRISKET OF BEEF STEWED.—Take any quantity of brisket of beef required, say eight or ten pounds, which cover with water, and stew till tender; bone the beef, and skim off the fat, strain the gravy, add a glass of port wine, and flavor with spice tied in a bag. Have boiled vegetables ready; cut them into squares, and garnish the beef from the gravy round it, and serve.

RUMP OF BEEF.—Cut the beef in pieces, half-boil them, put them into some beef broth or thin stock, unseasoned, and boil; when half done, stir some butter and flour moistened with broth in a stewpan over the fire until brown; put the beef into the pan with a dozen onions previously par-boiled, a glass of sherry, a bay leaf, a bunch of sweet herbs, parsley, pepper. and salt; stew till the beef and onions are quite done, then skim clean, cut an anchovy small, and put it with capers into the sauce; place the beef in the center of the dish, and garnish with the onions around it.

BEEF AND SAUER KRAUT.—Put about eight pounds of beef into cold water. When it comes to a boil, let it boil very fast for eight or ten minutes, not longer. Take it in a stewpan, covering it completely over with sauer kraut. Pour in a pint of thin gravy. Stew four hours, and serve with the gravy in a tureen or deep dish.

A BEEF STEW.—Take two or three pounds of the rump of beef, cut away all the fat and skin, and cut it into pieces about two or three inches square, put it into a stewpan, and pour on to it a quart of broth; then let it boil, and sprinkle in a little salt and pepper to taste; when it has boiled very gently, or simmered two hours, shred finely a large lemon, adding it to the gravy; add at pleasure two glasses of Madeira, or one of sherry or port, and serve.

BEEF HASHED.—Take the bones of the joint to be hashed; and break them small, then stew them in a very little water, with a bunch of sweet herbs and a few onions; roll a lump of butter in flour, brown it in a stewpan, pour the gravy to it, and add the meat to be hashed; two small onions in thin slices, a carrot also, and a little parsley shred finely; stew gently until the meat is hot through, and serve.

BUBBLE AND SQUEAK.—Sprinkle some slices of cold boiled beef with pepper, fry them with a bit of butter to a light brown; boil a cabbage, squeeze it quite dry, and chop it small, then take the beef out of the frying-pan and lay the cabbage in it, sprinkling a little salt and pepper over it; keep the pan moving over the fire for a few minutes; lay the cabbage in the middle of the dish, and the beef around it.

BEEF SAUSAGES.—To three pounds of beef, very lean, put one pound and a half of suet, and chop very finely; season with sage in powder, allspice, pepper, and salt; have skins thoroughly cleaned and force the meat into them.

TRIPE.—Take two pounds of fresh tripe, cleaned and dressed by the tripe-dresser, cut away the coarsest fat, and boil it for twenty minutes to half an hour, in equal parts of milk and water. Boil in the same water which boils the tripe four large onions; the onions should be put on the fire at least half an hour before the tripe is put in the stewpan, and then made into a rich onion sauce, which serve with the tripe. Another method of dressing tripe is by cutting it into slices; three eggs are beaten up with minced parsley, sweet herbs, onions, chopped exceedingly fine, and mushrooms. The tripe is dipped into this mixture, and fried in boiling lard.

Tripe can be stewed in gravy, in which put parsley, onions, and mushrooms. or in lieu of the latter. mushroom ketchup. Thicken the gravy with flour and butter. When the tripe is tender, it will be done. A lemon may be sent to table with it.

VEAL, THE FILLET.—The fillet derives much of its pleasant flavor from being stuffed. Veal, in itself, being nearly tasteless, the stuffing should be placed in the hollow from whence the bone is extracted, and the joint should be roasted a beautiful brown; it should be cooked gradually, as the meat, being solid, will require to be thoroughly done through without burning the outside; like pork, it is sufficiently indigestible, without being sent to table and eaten half cooked; a dish of boiled bacon or ham should accompany it to table, with the addition of a lemon. In roasting veal care must be taken that it is not at first placed too near the fire; the fat of a loin, one of the most delicate joints of veal, should be covered with greased paper; a fillet, also, should have on the caul until nearly done. The shoulder should be thoroughly boiled; when nearly done, dredge with flour, and produce a fine broth.

FILLET OF VEAL BOILED.—Bind it around with tape, put it in a floured cloth, and in cold water; boil very gently two hours and a half, or, if simmered, which is perhaps the better way, four hours will be necessary. It may be sent to table in bechemel, or with oyster sauce.

NECK OF VEAL.—May be boiled or roasted—the latter, only, if it be the best end—and sent to the table garnished nicely with vegetables; it may also be broiled in chops, but it is best in a pie; it is sometimes larded and stewed as follows: Lard it with square pieces of ham or bacon, which have been previously rubbed in a preparation of shalots, spices, pepper, and salt; place it in the stewpan with about three pints of white stock, adding a bay or laurel leaf, and a couple of onions; also add a dessertspoonful of brandy or whisky, and stew till tender, then dish the meat, strain the gravy, pour it over the joint, and serve.

VEAL CUTLETS.—The cutlets should be cut as handsomely as possible, and about three-quarters of an inch in thickness; before cooking, they should be well beaten with the blade of a chopper, if a proper beater be not at hand; then fry them a light brown, and send them up to table garnished with parsley, and rolls of thin-sliced, nicely fried bacon; they are with advantage coated, previous to cooking, with the yolk of an egg, and dredged with bread crumbs.

GALANTINE VEAL.—Take a large breast of veal; take off the shin bone, then take out the gristle called tendons, and all the rib bones; flatten it well, have ready some good forcemeat or sausage meat, and spread it all over with your forcemeat; then make a line of green gherkins, a line of red capsicums, a line of fat ham or bacon, some hard-boiled yolks of eggs, and a line of truffles; if you have any boiled calves' feet left from jelly stock, sprinkle it in with pieces of breast of fowl; sprinkle pepper and salt all over it, then roll it up tightly, and likewise do so in a cloth; tie it up tight; stew it for two hours or more; take it up, press it flat, and let it lie until quite cold; then take off the cloth. It will make an excellent cold dish.

EMINCEES.—Are made from dressed beef cut into very small dice; put fried or toasted bread sippets around the dish; a mashed potato or rice rim is the neatest way for this dish to be sent to table.

BREAST OF VEAL BOILED.—Put it into plenty of cold water, and let it come to a boil, clearing the scum as often as it rises; when it boils add a bunch of parsley, a few blades of mace, a small bunch of sweet herbs, twenty or thirty white peppers, and let it stew an hour and a quarter, then send to table with a nice piece of bacon, and parsley and butter.

BREAST OF VEAL RAGOUT.—Divide the breast lengthways in two, cutting each piece into portions of a reasonable size; then put them into a pan with boiling butter, and fry a clear brown; lay the pieces in a stew pan with sufficient veal broth to cover them, throw in a small fagot of sweet herbs and parsley, two onions, one large blade of mace, half a dessertspoonful of allspice, and the peel of a lemon; season with pepper and salt, cover close and stew an hour and a half, or longer if the meat requires it; then take it off and strain the gravy from the fat, keeping the vessel closely covered; in a small stew-pan put a little butter and flour, pour in the strained gravy gradually, let it come to a boil, remove any scum that may rise, pour in a glass of sherry or Madeira, two tablespoonfuls mushroom ketchup, and squeeze in the juice of half a lemon; boil it up, place the veal in a deep, hot dish, pour the gravy over it and serve.

SHOULDER OF VEAL.—Remove the knuckle and roast what remains, as the fillet; it may or may not be stuffed; if not stuffed, serve with oyster or mushroom sauce; if stuffed, with melted butter.

SHOULDER OF VEAL BONED AND STEWED.—Bone the shoulder and leave in the orifice a veal force-meat; roll and bind the shoulder; roast it an hour, then put it into a stewpan with good white or brown gravy, and stew four or five hours, regulating the time to the size of the joint; when it is done, strain the gravy to clear it of fat, and serve with forcemeat balls.

LOIN OF VEAL.—Divide the loin, roast the kidney, and place under the fat a toast, and serve swimming in melted butter. The chump end must be stuffed with the same stuffing as the fillet, and served with the same sauce; those who object to putting the stuffing in the joint may send it to table with balls of stuffing in the dish.

LOIN OF VEAL BOILED.—Take a loin about eight pounds, skewer down the flap without disturbing the kidney, put the loin into a kettle with enough cold water to cover it, and let it come gradually to a boil (it cannot boil too slowly); continue for two hours and a quarter, remove the scum as it rises, send it to table in bechemel, or with parsley and melted butter.

CALF'S FEET.—They should be very clean; boil them three hours, or until they are tender, then serve them with parsley and butter.

CALF'S HEART.—Stuffed and roasted precisely as beef heart.

CALF'S KIDNEY.—May be dressed as mutton or beef kidney, or mince it with some of the fat, add cayenne, white pepper, and salt, cover it with bread crumbs and with yolk of egg, make it up into balls, and fry in boiling fresh butter, drain them upon a sieve, and serve them upon fried parsley.

CALF'S HEAD FOR GRILL.—When the head is boiled sufficiently, draw out all the bones, and put it to cool, and then cut it (if not required whole) into square long pieces; egg and bread-crumb them as you would cutlets, only add some chopped sweet herbs, as well as parsley; put it in your oven to brown.

CALF'S HEAD BAKED.—Butter the head, and powder it with a seasoning composed of very fine bread crumbs, a few sweet herbs and sage, chopped very fine, cayenne, white pepper and salt. Divide the brains into several pieces, not too small, sprinkle them with bread crumbs, and lay them in the dish with the head. Stick a quantity of small pieces of butter over the head and in the eyes, throw crumbs over all, pour in three parts of the dish full of water, and bake in a fast oven two hours.

CALF'S BRAINS.—Wash them, remove the skin, and scald them. Dry them well, fry them in butter, and serve with mushroom sauce. Or, when cleaned and scalded, chop them finely, simmer them with mushrooms, onions, parsley, sage, and white sauce. Season highly, and serve with fried parsley and fried sippets.

CALF'S LIVER.—Lay the liver in vinegar for twelve hours, it will render it firm; then dip it in cold spring water and wipe it dry, cut it in even slices, sprinkle sweet herbs, crumbled finely, over it, and add pepper and salt; dredge with flour, and fry in boiling lard or butter—the last is preferable; remove the liver when fried a nice brown, pour away a portion of the fat, and pour in a cupful of water with a lump of butter well roiled in flour, in which a spoonful of vinegar and cayenne or lemon juice has been stirred; boil it up, keeping it stirred all the while, and serve the liver up in it; thin slices of hot fried bacon should be sent to table with it.

VEAL, CURRIED.—Cut the veal to be curried in small pieces—any part of veal, cooked or uncooked, that is palatable, will serve. Put in a stewpan six ounces of fresh butter, add to it half a pint of good white stock and one tablespoonful of curry powder, put to this the veal to be curried, cover down close, simmer for two hours, squeeze a quarter of a lemon into it, and serve with a dish of boiled rice.

HAUNCH OF MUTTON.—The haunch should be hung as long as possible without being tainted; it should be washed with vinegar every day while hanging, and dried thoroughly after each washing; if the weather be muggy, rubbing with sugar will prevent its turning sour; if warm weather, pepper and ground ginger rubbed over it will keep off the flies. When ready for roasting, paper the fat, and commence some distance from the fire; baste with milk and water first, and then, when the fat begins dripping, change the dish, and baste with its own dripping; half an hour previous to its being done, remove the paper from the fat, place it closer to the fire, baste well, and serve with currant jelly.

SADDLE OF MUTTON.—This joint, like the haunch, gains much of its flavor from hanging for some time; the skin should be taken off, but skewered on again until rather more than a quarter of an hour of its being done, then let it be taken off, dredge the saddle with flour, and baste well. The kidneys may be removed or remain, at pleasure, but the fat which is found within the saddle should be taken away previous to cooking.

LEG OF MUTTON ROASTED.—Like the haunch and saddle, should be hung before cooking, slowly roasted, and served with onion sauce or currant jelly.

LEG OF MUTTON BOILED.—Should be first soaked for an hour and a half in salt and water, care being taken that the water be not too salt, then wiped and boiled in a floured cloth; the time necessary for boiling will depend upon the weight; two hours or two hours and a half should be about the time; it should be served with mashed turnips, potatoes, greens and caper sauce, or brown cucumber, or oyster sauce.

MUTTON KIDNEYS BROILED.—Skin and split, without parting asunder; skewer them through the outer edge and keep them flat; lay the opened sides first to the fire, which should be clear and brisk; in four minutes turn them, sprinkle with salt and cayenne, and when done, which will be in three minutes afterward, take them from the fire, put a piece of butter inside them, squeeze some lemon juice over them, and serve as hot as possible.

FORE-QUARTER OF LAMB.—This is the favorite, and, indeed, the best joint. Do not put it too near the fire at first, and when it gets heated, baste it well; the fire should be quick, clear, but not fierce. The usual weight of a fore-quarter is between nine and eleven pounds, which will take two hours cooking; when it is done, separate the shoulder from the ribs, but before it is quite taken off, lay under a large lump of butter, squeeze a lemon, and season with pepper and salt; let it remain long enough to melt the butter, then remove the shoulder, and lay it on another dish.

STEAKS FROM A LOIN OF MUTTON are done in the same way, only trimming some of the fat off; cut thick, and stew instead of frying them.

MUTTON STEAKS.—The steaks are cut from the thick or fillet end of a leg of mutton, and dressed as rump-steaks.

MUTTON CHOPS BROILED.—Cut them from the best end of the loin, trim them nicely, removing fat or skin, leaving only enough of the former to make them palatable; let the fire be very clear before placing the chops on the gridiron, turn them frequently, taking care that the fork is not put into the lean part of the chop; season them with pepper and salt, spread fresh butter over each chop when nearly done, and send them to table on very hot plates.

FILLET OF MUTTON.—Choose a very large leg, cut from four to five inches in thickness from the large end, take out the bone, and in its place put a highly savored forcemeat, flour, and roast it for two hours; it may be sent to table with melted butter poured over it, or a rich brown gravy and red currant jelly.

HARICOT MUTTON.—In this dish remove the bones, leave the fat on, and cut each cutlet thick; fry them over a quick fire to brown; twelve cutlets will make this dish; put them into a proper sized stewpan with a little good second stock, pepper and salt, a little piece of sugar, cover it over and stew gently over a slow fire; when tender, strain off sufficient stock for the sauce.

HASH MUTTON. — Cut the cold mutton into slices as uniform in size as possible, flour them, pepper and salt them, put them into a stewpan with some gravy made of an onion stewed, with whole pepper and toasted bread, in a pint of water, to which a little walnut catsup has been added. This gravy should be stewed two hours before using. Do not let the hash boil; when it is done, add a little thickening of butter, flour, and water, if required, and serve up with sippets of toasted bread.

IRISH STEW.—Cut a neck of mutton as for the haricot; blanch the chops in water, then put them into another stewpan with four onions cut in slices, put to it a little of your second stock, and let it boil a quarter of an hour; have ready some potatoes pared, put them into the stewpan with the mutton, with salt and pepper. As some like the potatoes whole and some mashed, as to thicken the stew, you must boil them accordingly; dish the meat around, and the vegetables in the middle.

To MAKE A SCOTCH HAGGIS.—Take the stomach of a sheep. The washing and cleaning is of more consequence than all, as it will be a bad color and a bad taste if not well cleaned; when clean, turn it inside out, then let it lie for a day or two in salt and water. Blanch the liver, lights, and heart of the sheep, lay them in cold water, chop all very fine—the liver you had better grate; chop very finely a pound of the suet, and dry in the oven a pound of oatmeal; mix all this well together, season with pepper and salt, a little chopped parsley and onion; then sew up the bag; before you finish sewing it, add a few spoonfuls of good white stock; put it in a stewpan with a drainer; boil it in water, keeping it well covered all the time, and prick it all over with a small larding pin, to keep it from bursting; it will take several hours to boil; be careful in taking it up, and let your dish be large enough.

SHOULDER OF MUTTON.—Must be well roasted, and sent to table with the skin a nice brown, and serve with onion sauce.

LOIN OF MUTTON STEWED.—Remove the skin, bone it, roll it, then put it in a stewpan with a pint and a half of water, two dessertspoonfuls of pyroligneous acid, a piece of butter, sweet herbs, and an onion or two; when it has stewed nearly four hours, strain the gravy, add two spoonfuls of red wine, hot up, and serve with jelly.

BREAST OF MUTTON.—May be stewed in gravy until tender; bone it, score it, season well with cayenne, black pepper, and salt; boil it, and while cooking, skim the fat from the gravy in which it has been stewed, slice a few gherkins, and add with a dessertspoonful of mushroom catsup; boil it, and pour over the mutton when dished.

TO STEW A BRISKET OF LAMB.—Cut it into pieces, pepper and salt well, and stew in sufficient gravy to cover the meat until tender, then thicken the sauce, and pour in a glass of sherry; serve on a dish of stewed mushrooms.

SWEETBREADS.—Should be soaked in water, put for eight or ten minutes in boiling water, and then into clear cold spring water, to blanch. They may be cut in slices, or in dice, and put into fricassees of meat or ragouts, or they may be served as a separate dish.

SHEEP OR LAMB'S TROTTERS.—Get a dozen or two of trotters, stew them for several hours, until all the bones will come from them; save the liquor; do not break the skin, stuff them with good quenells or forcemeat; return them again into the stock, boil them about fifteen minutes, and glaze them; sauce is good with them, or you may fry them with butter.

TO ROAST A LEG OF LAMB.—The rules laid down for roast mutton must be scrupulously observed with respect to lamb; let it roast gradually, and commence a distance from the fire; a leg of five pounds will take an hour and a quarter, one of six pounds will take an hour and a half,

To Boil a Leg of Lamb.—Put in sufficient clear cold soft water to cover it, let it remain half an hour; a tablespoonful of vinegar or half a handful of salt may be thrown in; put it into a thin white cloth which has been floured, and boil it; a good-sized bundle of sweet herbs may be thrown into the saucepan; if six pounds, it will be done in an hour and a half; serve with spinach or French beans; if sent to table cold, tastefully lay handsome sprigs of parsley about it; it may, while hot, be garnished with parsley, with thin slices of lemon laid round the dish.

To Roast a Sucking Pig.—A sucking pig should be dressed as soon after being killed as practicable. When scalded and prepared for cooking, lay in the belly a stuffing of bread, sage and onions, pepper and salt, with a piece of butter, then sew it up, rub the skin of the pig with butter, skewer the legs back, that, roasting, the inside as well as outside of the pig may be thoroughly browned. It must be put to a quick fire, but at such a distance as to roast gradually, and a coating of flour should be dredged over it, that it may not blister, or it should not be left a minute; if floured, when the pig is done scrape the flour off with a wooden or very blunt knife, and rub it with a buttered cloth; cut off the head, and dividing it, take out the brains, mix them with a little gravy or bread sauce; divide the pig in half from the neck to tail, and lay each inside flap upon the dish, so that the two edges of the back touch; place each half of the head with the outer side uppermost at each end of the dish, and an ear on each side; the gravy should be poured in the dish hot, and the whole served as hot as possible.

A Leg of Pork Roasted.—Score the skin with a sharp penknife; a little fresh butter is sometimes rubbed over the skin to make it brown and crisp without blistering. Chop some sage that has been scalded very fine, add to it an onion parboiled, mix some bread crumbs and a small portion of finely chopped apple; mix all together, season with pepper and salt, make an incision by separating the skin from the fat in the under and fillet end of the leg, and place the stuffing there; serve up with apple sauce. The time of roasting will depend upon the size of the leg.

A Leg of Pork Boiled.—After having been salted it should be washed in clean cold water, and scraped thoroughly white and clean preparatory to cooking; it should then be put into a floured cloth, and into cold water on the fire; when the rind is quite tender the pork will be done. Let the water be well skimmed, and serve with such vegetables as are in season. Should the joint be large, allow a quarter of an hour to each pound, with an additional twenty minutes from the time it boils.

Spare Rib.—A spare rib will take two hours and a half to roast, unless very large, and then three hours will be required to cook it thoroughly; while roasting, baste with butter and dredge with flour, pound some sage, and powder the spare rib with it about twenty minuter before it is done; a pinch of salt may be added.

Boiled Pork—of All Kinds.—The leg you must skin the same as ham, and dish it back part upward and glaze it; place a ruffle at the knuckle; use for sauce, sauer kraut, or stewed red cabbage; peas pudding to all pork when boiled.

Pig's Cheek—A Half One.—Boil and trim in the shape of ham, and if very fat carve it as a cockle-shell; glaze it well, or put bread crumbs and brown them; sauce as before.

PORK CHOPS OR STEAKS.—Cut from the best end of the loin, or from the chumy or leg if steaks; remove the fat and skin and turn them frequently and quickly while broiling; sprinkle them with salt when nearly done, and rub with a little fresh butter previous to serving; if for a side-dish garnish with crisped parsley.

PIG'S HEAD BAKED.—Let it be divided, and thoroughly cleaned; take out the brains, trim the snout and ears, bake it an hour and a half, wash the brains thoroughly, blanch them, beat them up with an egg, pepper and salt, some finely chopped or pounded sage, and a small piece of butter; fry them, or brown them, before the fire; serve with the head.

PIG'S HEAD BOILED.—This is the more profitable dish, though not so pleasant to the palate; it should first be salted, which is usually done by the pork butcher; it should be boiled gently an hour and a quarter; serve with vegetables.

TO BAKE A HAM.—Put the ham in soak previous to dressing it; if an old one, two hours will be required, but if not very old, an hour will suffice. Wipe it very dry, and cover it with a paste about an inch in thickness. The edges being first moistened, must be drawn together, and made to adhere, or the gravy will escape. Bake it in a regular well-heated oven; it will take from three to six hours, according to its weight; when done, remove the paste and then the skin. This must be done when the ham is hot. If well baked, and not too salt, it will prove of finer flavor than if boiled.

HAM RASHERS, OR SLICES.—May be toasted, broiled, or fried, and served with spinach and poached eggs, or boiled green peas. Stewed with green peas, or cut in thin slices, divided in four pieces, each piece rolled and fastened with a skewer, roasted in a Dutch oven, and served with peas. They should, in all cases, be cut in even thickness, and cooked without injuring the color. Bacon may be dressed in the same variety.

To Broil Bacon.—Make up a sheet of paper in the drippingpan, cut your bacon into thin slices, cut off the rind, lay the bacon on the paper, put it over the gridiron, set it over a slow fire, and it will broil clearly.

Bacon and Cabbage.—Boil some fine streaked part of bacon with a little stock, and the ends of eight or ten sausages; boil in the same stock some white cabbages for two hours, adding salt and spice, and serve very hot; place your sausages and cabbage around the dish, and the bacon in the middle.

Bacon and Eggs.—Take a quarter of a pound of streaked bacon, cut it into thin slices, and put them into a stewpan over a slow fire, taking care to turn them frequently; then pour the melted fat of the bacon into a dish, break over it seven or eight eggs, add two spoonfuls of gravy, and a little salt and pepper, and stew the whole over a slow fire, pass a salamander over it, and serve.

Bacon Toast.—Cut some thin slices of bread, about two or three inches long, and some streaked bacon in small pieces, dip them into a raw egg beaten up with shred parsley, green onions, shallots, and pepper; fry over a slow fire, and serve with clear sauce and a little vinegar.

Turkey Roast.—It is stuffed with either sausage meat or fillet of veal stuffing. While roasting, a piece of paper should be placed over the part stuffed, as, being bulky, it will catch the fire and become scorched, but keep the heat well to the breast, in order that it may be as well done as the rest of the bird. Baste well, and froth it up. Serve with gravy in the dish, and bread sauce in a tureen. To the sausage meat, if used, add a few bread crumbs and a beaten egg. Turkey is sometimes stuffed with truffles; they are prepared thus: they must be peeled, and chopped, and pounded in a mortar, in quantities of a pound and a half; rasp the same weight of the fat of bacon, and mix it with the truffles; stuff the turkey with it; this stuffing is usually placed in the turkey two days previous to cooking, it is supposed to impart a flavor to the flesh of the fowl. Cut thin slices of fat bacon, and place over the breast of the turkey. Secure it with half a sheet of clean white paper, and roast. Two hours will roast it.

TURKEY BOILED.—A hen bird is considered the best. It may be stuffed with truffles, or sausage meat. Boil it in a clean floured cloth; throw some salt into the water in which it is boiled. Cover cloth, and simmer for two hours, removing the scum frequently. Serve with white sauce, or parsley and butter.

TURKEY HASHED.—Cut up the remains of a roasted turkey, put it into a stewpan with half a gill of sherry, shallots, truffles. mushroons. chopped parsley, salt, pepper, and a little stock; boil half an hour, and reduce to a thick sauce. When ready, add a pound of anchovies. and a squeeze of lemon. Skim the sauce free from fat, and serve all together.

TURKEY LEGS BROILED.—Braise some undressed legs of turkey until tender, dip them in melted butter, or clear salad oil, broil them a fine brown color, and serve with sauce.

To Roast a Goose.—There are many modes of stuffing; for one mode, take two moderate sized onions, and boil them rapidly ten minutes, then chop them finely, mince sage to the quantity of half the onion, add of powdered bread twice as much as of onion, pepper and salt it, introducing a little cayenne, and then bind it with the beaten yolk of an egg. Potatoes mashed are sometimes introduced, but not frequently, into the body; they should be mashed with floury potatoes mixed with a little fresh butter and cream, rather highly seasoned with cayenne and salt. Both ends of the goose should be secured when trussed, that the seasoning may not escape. It should be roasted before a quick fire, and kept constantly basted ; it will take from an hour and a half to an hour and three-quarters; serve with a rich brown gravy and apple sauce. Previous to sending to table, a flavoring may be made as follows: To a dessert-spoonful of made mustard, add a quarter of a tea-spoonful of cayenne pepper, about the same quantity of salt, mix it evenly with a glass of port wine, and two glasses of rich gravy, make it hot, cut a slit in the apron of the goose, and pour it through just previously to serving.

To Roast Ducks.—Clean the insides thoroughly with a little warm water, and stuff them with the same stuffing as for geese, using a little more bread for the sake of mildness; roast them before a brisk fire, but not too close, and baste very frequently; they will take from half an hour to an hour, according to the age and size; when the breast plumps, they will be just done; serve them with a rich brown gravy.

To Boil Ducks.—Salt them for about thirty hours previous to cooking; flour a clean white

cloth and boil them in it, a moderate sized duck
will sake about an hour's boiling; make a rich
onion sauce with milk, and send it to table with
the duck. When the duck is boiled fresh it may
be stuffed as for roasting, and served with the
same description of gravy.

STEWED DUCK.—The ducks should be cut into
joints, and laid in a stewpan with a pint of good
gravy, let it come to a boil, and, as the scum rises,
remove it; season with salt and cayenne, and let
them stew gently three-quarters of an hour, mixing
smoothly two teaspoonfuls of fine ground rice, with
a glass of port, which stir into the gravy, and let
it have seven or eight minutes to amalgamate with
it, then dish and send to table very hot.

WILD DUCKS, OR TEAL.—You must be very particular in not roasting these birds too much; a
duck about fifteen minutes, with a good fire; baste
them very frequently; teal will, of course, take less
time, but your fire and motion of the spit must be
attended to, and when you dish it, draw your knife
four times down the breast; have ready a little hot
butter, and juice of a lemon, cayenne pepper, a
little dust of sugar, a glass of port wine; pour it
all hot, at the last minute, over your ducks; the
remainder left of these birds the next day makes
excellent salmi or hash, taking care of all the
gravy that may remain.

ROAST FOWLS.—If nicely trussed, make a stuffing of butter and some pepper; dry up the butter
with a few bread crumbs; baste it well, adding
flour and salt before you take it from the fire. If
approved of, stuff the fowl with some good sausage
meat, truffles, or chestnuts.

BOILED FOWLS.—Flour a white cloth, and put
the fowls in cold water; let them simmer for three-

quarters of an hour; serve with parsley and butter, or oyster or celery sauce. The fowls may be covered with a white sauce if sent cold to table, and garnished with colored calf's foot jelly of the hue of beetroot.

BROILED FOWL.—Separate the back of the fowl, and lay the two sides open; skewer the wings as for roasting, season well with pepper and salt, and broil; send to table with the inside of the fowl to the surface of the dish, and serve mushroom sauce; it is an admirable breakfast dish when a journey is to be performed.

MADE DISHES OF POULTRY.—Partly roast the fowl, cut it up, detach the wings and legs, carefully dividing side bones, neck bones, breast and back, in as handsome pieces as possible; take eight or ten large onions, which, cut in slices of moderate thickness, make in a stewpan a layer of the sliced onion with some chopped parsley, then lay upon it some of the fowl, again a layer of the onion and parsley, until the whole of the fowl and onion are used; place two bay leaves, about as much salt as would fill a large teaspoon, four tablespoonfuls of olive oil, or, if that is not to the palate, substitute cream; it should simmer gently until it is done and then be dished, the onion in the middle; serve with a little sauce.

AN INDIAN PILAU.—Truss a fowl as for boiling, pass it a few minutes in the oven, raising it up with bacon or buttered paper; fry some onions, a few bruised coriander seeds, and a few cardamom seeds whole. fry a nice light color four onions cut in slices, adding to this a gill or more of cream, when all fried in a little butter; put in your fowl with some good veal stock, have ready some rice boiled in milk for two minutes, skim it off and add it to the fowl, frequently looking at it, and moving it to keep it from sticking or burning; let your fowl stew for a quarter of an hour before you add the rice, and do not let the rice get mashed; season with cayenne pepper and salt, putting all the rice and liquor around the fowl. You can use rabbits, chickens, quails, or veal instead of fowl, the same way.

CHICKENS BOILED.—Care should be taken to select the chickens plump, or they form a meager dish; they should receive much attention in the boiling; they require less time than a fowl, and are sent to table with white sauce, and garnished with tufts of white broccoli.

CHICKENS PULLED.—Remove the skin carefully from a cold chicken, then pull the flesh from the bones; preserving it as whole as you can. Flour them well and fry them a nice brown in fresh butter; draw them, and stew in a good gravy well-seasoned; thicken a short time before serving with flour and butter, and add the juice of half a lemon.

PIGEONS ROASTED.—Veal stuffing for pigeons, it improves the flavor; they must be fresh and well cleaned; butter and parsley may be served with them; but parsley alone as a stuffing, though frequently used, is by no means so palatable as the veal stuffing, or one made with veal, the fat of bacon, and the crumbs of bread soaked in milk, and well seasoned. They are sometimes stuffed with truffles, or chestnuts and bacon, as turkey, covered with thin slices of fat bacon enwrapped in vine leaves.

PIGEON—BROILED.—Split the backs, season them highly, lay them over a clear brisk fire, and serve with mushroom sauce.

PIGEONS STEWED.—Take a white cabbage, cut it as if for pickling, then rinse it in clear cold water, drain it well, and put it into a saucepan with equal quanties of milk and water, boil it, strain off the milk, and take a portion of the cabbage and lay it in a stewpan; soak the pigeons for half an hour in cold milk and water, season them well with salt and pepper, adding a little cayenne; then place them in the stewpan with the cabbage, cover them over with what remains, add some white broth, stew slowly until the pigeons are tender, thicken with a little cream, flour, and butter, let it boil, and serve up the pigeon with a puree of the cabbage.

TO POT PIGEONS.—Season them well with pepper, cayenne, a little mace, and salt, pack them closely in a pan, cover them with butter, and bake them; let them get cold, then take off the fat; and put the pigeons into pots, pouring melted butter over them.

WOOD PIGEONS.—May be dressed exactly as tame pigeons, save that they require less time in the cooking, and the gravy or sauce should be richer and of higher flavor.

VENISON—THE HAUNCH.—The haunch of venison, when about to be roasted, should be washed in warm milk and water, and dried with a clean cloth. During the time it is at the fire, do not be afraid of basting it too much; if it be a buck haunch, and large, it will take nearly four hours; if comparatively small, three hours and a half will suffice; if a doe haunch, three hours and a quarter will be enough. Dish it and serve, but let there be nothing with it in the dish; the gravy should be sent to table in its proper dish, accompanied by currant jelly.

HASHED VENISON.—Cut and trim some nice thin slices of venison, fat and lean; have a nice brown sauce made from the bones in scrag of the venison, put the meat you have cut into this sauce with the gravy that has run from the venison, and a glass of port wine. Cut up some of the fat into pieces an inch thick, put the fat in a stewpan, and some hot stock upon them; when you have dished up your hash, which should be in a hot water dish, with a holey spoon, take out the fat, and sprinkle it all over the hash; send up currant jelly.

PARTRIDGES.—Should not be stuffed. Grate bread crumbs into a shallow dish, place them before the fire to brown, shaking them occasionally, and send them to table with the birds.

PARTRIDGES—BROILED.—Let the partridge hang until longer would make it offensive, then split it, and take a soft clean cloth and remove all the moisture inside and out; lay it upon a gridiron over a very clear fire, and spread a little salt and cayenne over it. When it is done, which will be in twenty minutes, rub a little butter over it, and send it to table with mushroom sauce.

STUFFING FOR A HARE.—After having either scraped or scalded the liver, scrape some fat bacon, a little suet, some parsley, thyme, knotted-marjoram, a little shallot, a few crumbs of bread, pepper and salt, a few grains of nutmeg, beat it all well in a mortar with one egg, but if your hare is boned it will take more. You can dress a boned hare two ways: either taking each bone out but the head and the point of the tail; but this will not keep so good a shape as if you only took out the back and rib bones, leaving the shoulders and legs on; this way, when stuffed, will keep its shape best.

PLOVERS.—These birds must not be drawn; roast them before a brisk fire, but at a distance, and serve on toast with melted butter.

WOODCOCKS AND SNIPES.—Should not be drawn, but have toast as for grouse under them, passing out the tail, and chop it and spread it on the bird; lay them under the heads in the dripping pan.

RABBITS.—You will roast the same as hares; and if required to be stuffed—melted butter, chopped parsley, and the liver chopped, pepper and salt.

BOILED RABBITS.—A rabbit should boil only twenty minutes, and boil slowly; if larger than common, an extra ten minutes may be allowed; it should be sent to table smothered in onion sauce, and the water should be kept free from scum. It is trussed for boiling differently to what it is for roasting.

RABBIT WITH ONIONS.—Truss your rabbit, and lay it in cold water; if for boiling, pour the gravy of onions over it, and if you have a white stock-pot on, boil it in that.

VEGETABLES, SALADS, ETC.

CHARTREUSE OF VEGETABLES.—Line a plain mold with bacon; have ready some half-done carrots, turnips, French beans cut long with a French cutter, all the same length, place them prettily round the mold, until you get to the top, and fill in the middle with mashed potatoes, cauliflower, spinach, or some veal forcemeat; put it on to steam, turn it out, and put asparagus or mushroom sauce round it.

ASPARAGUS.—Let the stalks be lightly but well scraped, and as they are done, be thrown into cold water; when all are finished, fasten them into bundles of equal size; put them into boiling water, throw in a handful of salt, boil until the end of the stalk becomes tender, which will be about half an hour; cut a round of bread, and toast it a clear brown, moisten it with the water in which the asparagus was boiled, and arrange the stalks with the white ends outward. A good melted butter must accompany it to table. Asparagus should be dressed as soon after it has been cut as practicable.

FRENCH BEANS.—When very young the ends and stalks only should be removed, and as they are done, thrown into cold spring water; when to be dressed. put them in boiling water which has been salted with a small quantity of common salt; in a quarter of an hour they will be done, the criterion for which is when they become tender; the saucepan should be left uncovered, there should not be too much water, and they should be kept boiling rapidly. When they are at their full growth, the ends and strings should be taken off. and the beans divided lengthwise and across, or, according to the present fashion. slit diagonally or aslant. A small piece of soda a little larger than a small-sized pea, if put into the boiling water with the beans. or with any vegetables, will preserve that beautiful green which is so desirable for them to possess when placed upon the table.

FRENCH BEANS, SALAD.—Boil them simply, drain them, and let them cool; put them in a dish, and garnish with parsley. pimpernel, and tarragon, and dress like other salads.

STEWED BEANS —Boil them in water in which a lump of butter has been placed; preserve them as white as you can; chop a few sweet herbs with some parsley very fine, then stew them in a pint of the water in which the leaves have been boiled, and to which a quarter of a pint of cream has been added; stew until quite tender, then add the beans and stew five minutes, thickening with butter and flour.

BEANS BOILED.—Boil in salt and water with a bunch of savory, drain, and then put them into a stewpan, with five spoonfuls of sauce tournee reduced, the yolk of three eggs, and a little salt; then add a piece of fresh butter, and stir it constantly till of a proper thickness.

WINDSOR BEANS.—They should be young, and shelled only just previous to cooking; salt the water in which they are to be cooked, and, when boiling, throw in the beans; when tender, drain in a cullender, and send to table with plain melted butter, or parsley and butter. They usually accompany bacon or boiled pork to table.

HARICOT BEANS.—Take two handfuls of the white beans, and let them lie in boiling water until the skins come off; putting them in cold water as you do them, then take them out, and put them in a stewpan with some good stock, and boil them until nearly to a glaze; then add some good brown sauce to them, shaking them about; season with sugar, salt, and pepper.

BEET ROOTS.—Cut in equal-sized slices some beet root, boiled or baked, of a good color, make it hot between two plates in the oven, dish it as you would cutlets, round; make a good piquant sauce, boil some button onions white and tender, and throw them in the middle of the dish with the sauce.

CABBAGES.—A full-grown or summer cabbage should be well and thoroughly washed; before cooking, cut it into four pieces, boil rapidly, with the saucepan uncovered, half an hour; a young cabbage will take only twenty minutes, but it must be boiled very rapidly; a handful of salt should be thrown in the water before the cabbage is put in.

CABBAGE RED.—They are mostly stewed to eat with ham, bacon, or smoked sausages, though sometimes without any meat; they are very strong eating, and should be first scalded, then stewed with butter, pepper, salt, and cloves, and vinegar added to it just before serving; they are considered wholesome in veal broth for consumptives, but are mostly pickled.

CAULIFLOWER, TO BOIL.—Trim it neatly, and let it soak at least an hour in cold water, then put it into boiling water, in which a handful of salt has been thrown; let it boil, occasionally skimming the water. If the cauliflower is small, it will only take fifteen minutes; if large, twenty minutes may be allowed; do not let it remain after it is done, but take it up, and serve immediately. If the cauliflower is to be preserved white, it ought to be boiled in milk and water, or a little flour should be put into the water in which it is boiled, and melted butter should be sent to table with it.

GREEN PEAS.—A delicious vegetable, a grateful accessory to many dishes of a more substantial nature. Green peas should be sent to table *green;* no dish looks less tempting than peas if they wear an autumnal aspect. Peas should also be young, and as short a time as possible should be suffered to elapse between the periods of shelling and boiling. If it is a matter of consequence to send them to table in perfection, these rules must be strictly observed. They should be as near of a size as a discriminating eye can arrange them; they should then be put in a cullender, and some cold water suffered to run through them in order to wash them; then, having the water in which they are to be boiled slightly salted, and boiling rapidly, pour in the peas; keep the saucepan uncovered, and keep them boiling swiftly until tender; they will take about twenty minutes, barely so long, unless older than they should be; drain completely, pour them into the tureen in which they are to be served, and in the center put a slice of butter, and when it has melted, stir round the peas gently, adding pepper and salt; serve as quickly and as hot as possible.

How to Cook Potatoes.—Potatoes should always be boiled in their "jackets;" peeling a potato before boiling is offering a premium for water to run through it and making them waxy and unpalatable; they should be thoroughly washed and put into cold water.

To Boil New Potatoes.—The sooner the new potatoes are cooked after being dug, the better they will eat; clear off all the loose skins with a coarse towel and cold water; when they are thoroughly clean, put them into scalding water; a quarter of an hour or twenty minutes will be found sufficient to cook them; strain off the water dry, sprinkle a little salt over the potatoes, and send them to table. If very young, melted butter should accompany them.

Roasted Potatoes.—Clean thoroughly; nick a small piece out of the skin, and roast in the oven of the range; a little butter is sometimes rubbed over the skin to make them crisp.

FRIED POTATOES.—Remove the peel from an uncooked potato. After it has been thoroughly washed, cut the potatoes into thin slices, and lay them in a pan with some fresh butter; fry gently a clear brown, then lay them one upon the other in a small dish, and send to table as an *entremets*.

SPINACH.—The leaves of the spinach should be picked from the stems; it should then be well washed in clean cold water, until the whole of the dirt and grit is removed; three or four waters should be employed, it will not otherwise be got thoroughly clean: let it drain in a sieve, or shake it in a cloth, to remove the clinging water. Place it in a saucepan with boiling water—there should be very little; it will be done in ten minutes; squeeze out the water, chop the spinach finely, seasoning well with pepper and salt; pour three or four large spoonfuls of gravy over it, place it before the fire until much of the moisture has evaporated, and then serve.

LETTUCE AND ENDIVES.—Are better, I think, only cut into pieces or into quarters, and dished neatly round, but they must be done in some good stock, and not put into thick sauce; but when you take them out after being done, you will press and form them, then boil down their liquor to a glaze, which will, when added to your already thick sauce, give the desired flavor; glaze the quarters before dishing them; pour the sauce under and around.

PASTRY, TARTS, ETC.

PUFF PASTE.—One pound of butter, salt or fresh, and one pound of flour, will make a good dish of patty-cases, or a large case for a vol-au-vent, and the remainder into a good dish of second course pastry. Put your flour upon your board, work finely in with your hands lightly a quarter of the butter, then add water sufficient to make it the stiffness or softness of the remainder of the butter; each should be the same substance; work it up smooth, then roll it out longways half an inch thick; and place the remainder of the butter cut in slices half way on the paste; dust flour lightly over it, and double it up; press it down with your rolling-pin, letting it lie a few minutes, then roll it three times, thinner each time, letting it lie a few minutes between each roll, keeping it free from sticking to the board or rolling-pin. This paste is ready for patty-cases, or vol-au-vent, or meat pies.

BEEFSTEAK PIE.—Take some good steaks, beat them with a rolling pin, season them with pepper and salt; fill a dish with them, adding as much water as will half fill it, then cover it with a good crust, and bake it well.

COLD VEAL OR CHICKEN PIE.—Lay a crust into a shallow tart dish, and fill it with the following mixture: Shred cold veal or fowl, and half the quantity of ham, mostly lean; put to it a little cream; season with white and cayenne pepper, salt, a little nutmeg, and a small piece of shallot chopped as fine as possible; cover with crust, and turn it out of the dish when baked, or bake the crust with a piece of bread to keep it hollow, and warm the mince with a little cream, and pour in.

EGG MINCE PIE.—Take six eggs, boil them hard, then shred them very small; take twice the quantity of suet, and chop it very fine; well wash and pick a pound of currants, shred fine the peel of a lemon, add them with the juice, six spoonfuls of sweet wine, mace, nutmeg, sugar, a very small quantity of salt, orange, lemon, and citron, candied. Cover with a very light paste.

LEMON MINCE PIES.—Take a large lemon, squeeze the juice from it, and boil the outside till it becomes soft enough to beat to a smash; put to it three large apples, four ounces of suet, the same of sugar, and half a pound of currants; add the juice of the lemon, and some candied fruit, the same as for other pies. Make a short crust, and fill the patty-pans in the usual way.

MINCE PIES WITHOUT MEAT.—Take of currants, apples chopped fine, moist sugar, and suet well chopped, a pound of each; a quarter of a pound of raisins stoned and chopped small, the juice of four Seville oranges, the juice of two lemons, the rind of one shred fine, nutmeg and mace to suit the palate, and a glass of brandy. Mix all together, put it in a pan, and keep it closely tied up.

MUTTON PIE.—Cut steaks from a neck or loin of mutton that has hung, beat them, and remove some of the fat, season with salt and pepper, and a little onion; put a little water at the bottom of the dish and a little paste on the edge, then cover with a moderately thick paste, or raise small pies, and break each bone in two to shorten it, season and cover it over, pinching the edge. When they come out of the oven, pour into each a little second stock.

PORK PIE.—Cut a piece of the loin of pork into chops; remove the rind and bone, cut it into pieces, season well with pepper and salt, cover with puff paste. and bake the pie. When ready to be served, put in some cullis, with the essence of two onions mixed with a little mustard.

SQUAB PIE.—Cut apples as for other pies. and lay them in rows with mutton chops, shred onions, and sprinkle it among them, and also some sugar.

YORKSHIRE PUDDING.—Mix together a spoonful of flour, a pint of milk. and one egg well beaten, add a spoonful of salt, and a little ginger grated; put this mixture in a square pan buttered, and when browned by baking under the meat, turn the other side upward, to be browned also; serve it cut in pieces, and arranged upon a dish. If you require a richer pudding, increase the number of eggs.

APPLE DUMPLINGS.—Pare a few good-sized baking apples, and roll out some paste, divide it into as many pieces as you have apples, cut two rounds from each, and put an apple under each piece, and put the other over, join the edges, tie them in cloths, and boil them.

APPLE TART.—Take some good baking apples, pare, core, and cut them into small pieces; place them in a dish lined with puff paste, strew over pounded sugar, cinnamon, mace, nutmeg, cloves, and lemon peel chopped small; then add a layer of apples, then spice, and so on till the dish is full; pour a glass and a half of white wine over the whole, cover with puff paste. and bake it. When done, raise the crust, stir in two ounces of fresh butter, and two eggs well beaten, replace the crust, and serve either hot or cold.

RASPBERRY TART. - Put some raspberries in a patty-pan lined with thin puff paste, strew in some finely-sifted sugar, cover with puff paste, and bake it; when done, take off the top, and pour in half a pint of cream, previously mixed with the yolks of two or three eggs. and sweetened with a little sugar; then return the tart to the oven for five or six minutes.

STRAWBERRY TART.—Put into a basin two quarts of the best scarlet strawberries picked, add half a pint of cold clarified sugar, the same quantity of Madeira, with the juice of two lemons, mix all well without breaking the strawberries, and put them into a puff paste previously baked; keep them very cool.

OYSTER PATTIES.—Line some small patty-pans with a fine puff paste, put a piece of bread into each, cover with paste, and bake them. While they are baking, take some oysters, beard them, and cut the remainder up into small pieces; place them in a tosser, with a very small portion of grated nutmeg. a very little white pepper and salt, a morsel of lemon peel cut as small as possible, a little cream, and a little of the oyster liquor; simmer it a few minutes, then remove the bread from the patties and put in the mixture.

MEAT PATTIES.—The patty-pans should not be too large; make a puff paste, put a layer at the bottom of the tins. put in forcemeat, and cover with puff paste, bake them a light brown, turn them out. If for a small dinner, five patties, or seven for a large dinner, will suffice for a side dish.

RICE PANCAKES.—To half a pound of rice put two-thirds of a pint of water; boil it to a jelly; when cold, add to it eight eggs. a pint of cream, a little salt and nutmeg, and half a pound of butter melted; mix well, adding the butter last, and working it only so much as will make the batter sufficiently thick. Fry them in lard, but employ as little as it is possible to fry them with.

FRITTERS are made of batter, the same as pancakes. Drop a small quantity into the pan, have ready apples pared, sliced, and cored, lay them in the batter and fry them; they may also be made with sliced lemon or currants, the latter is particularly palatable. They should be sent to table upon a folded napkin in the dish; any sweetmeat or ripe fruit will make fritters.

APPLE FRITTERS.—Take two or three large russeting apples, pare them thin, cut them half an inch thick, lay them on a pie-dish, pour brandy over them, and let them lie two hours; make a thick batter, using two eggs; have clean lard and make it quite hot; fry two at a time, a nice light brown; put them on the back of a sieve on paper, sift pounded sugar over them, glaze them with a shovel or salamander; dish on a napkin. After they are cut in slices, take out the core with a small round cutter.

INDIAN CORN CAKES.—Mix a quart of Indian meal with a handful of wheat flour, stir in a quart of warm milk, a teaspoonful of salt, and two spoonfuls of yeast; stir alternately into the milk, the meal and three well beaten eggs; when light, bake as buckwheat cakes, on a griddle; send them to the table hot. Should the batter sour, stir in a little saleratus dissolved in luke-warm water, letting it set half an hour before baking,

BEST SPONGE CAKE.—Take one coffee-cupful of sugar, and four eggs; beat them to a cream; add a piece of saleratus as large as a pea dissolved in a teaspoonful of milk; also a little nutmeg and essence of lemon; stir in carefully a coffee-cup of flour. Bake in a quick oven.

A LIGHT CAKE.—Take a pint bowl full and a half of sugar, one and a half cups of butter rubbed in two pint bowls of flour, two cups of sour cream, a teaspoonful of saleratus, tablespoonful of rose water, four eggs well beaten, and a little nutmeg.

COMPOSITION CAKE.—Take four cups of flour, four of sugar, two cups of butter, five eggs, half a pint of cream, teaspoonful of saleratus, spice to suit your taste. Beat all well together, and bake in a butter tin or in cups.

INDIAN GRIDDLE CAKE.—Take one pint of Indian meal and one cup of flour, a little salt and ginger, a tablespoonful of molasses, a teaspoonful of saleratus, sour milk enough to make a stiff batter. Bake them on a griddle like buckwheat cakes.

COMMON PLUM CAKE.—Mix five cups of butter with ten cups of flour, five cups of sugar; add six cups stoned raisins. a little cinnamon and mace finely powdered, half a cup of good new yeast put into a pint of new milk, warm and mix the dough; let it stand till it is light.

POUND CAKE.—One pound dried sifted flour, the same of loaf sugar, and the whites of twelve eggs and the yolks of seven. Beat the butter to a cream, add the sugar by degrees, then the eggs and flour; beat it all well together for an hour, mixing a teaspoonful of rose water, a little nutmeg or cinnamon, two cups of cream, and a teaspoonful of saleratus. To be baked in a quick oven.

TEA CAKES.—A quart of flour, one pint of sour cream, teaspoonful saleratus, two cups of molasses, a little cinnamon and salt; make a stiff paste, and bake it in a moderate oven.

BREAKFAST BUTTER CAKES.—One quart of sour milk, one teaspoonful saleratus, a little salt, one and a half cups of boiled rice. two table-spoonfuls molasses or half cup of sugar, a little ginger, and flour enough to make a stiff batter.

BUCKWHEAT CAKES.—Take one quart of buck-wheat meal, half a cup of new yeast, a teaspoonful of saleratus, a little salt, and sufficient new milk or cold water to make a thick batter. Put it in a warm place to rise. When it has risen sufficiently, bake it on a griddle or in a spider. The griddle must be well buttered, and the cakes are better to be small and thin.

PLAIN INDIAN CAKES.—Take a quart of sifted Indian meal, sprinkle a little salt over it, mix it with scalding water, stirring; bake on a tin stove oven. Indian cake is made with buttermilk, or sour milk, with a little cream or butter rubbed into the meal, and a teaspoonful of saleratus.

BUTTER CAKES FOR TEA.—Beat two eggs, put them in half pint of milk, and a teacup of cream, with half a teaspoonful of saleratus dissolved in the cream. a little salt, cinnamon and rose-water if you like, stir in sifted flour till the batter is smooth and thick. Bake them on a griddle or in a pan. But-ter the pan well, drop the batter in small round cakes and quite thin. They must be turned and nicely browned. Lay them on a plate with a little butter between each layer.

CREAM CAKES.—One quart of flour, one pint of cream, a little sour cream, one teaspoonful of saleratus dissolved in the sour cream. If the flour is not made sufficiently wet with the above quantity of cream, add more sweet cream.

ROLLS.—Rub into a pound of flour half a teacup-ful of butter; add half a teacup of sweet yeast, a little salt, and sufficient warm milk to make a stiff dough; cover and put it where it will be kept warm, and it will rise in two hours. Then make into rolls or round cakes. They will bake in a quick oven in fifteen minutes.

CUP CAKE.—Take one cup of butter, two cups of sugar. three cups of flour, and four eggs. Teaspoonful of saleratus, nutmeg and rose water.

TEA CAKE.—To four cups of flour add three cups of sugar, three eggs, one cup of butter, one cup of milk, and one spoonful of dissolved pearlash.

INDIAN CAKE.—Take three cups of Indian meal, two cups of flour, one half a teacup of molasses, a little salt, one teaspoonful of saleratus, and mix them with cold water.

LOAF CAKE.—Two pounds of flour, half a pound of sugar, quarter of butter, three eggs, one gill of milk, half a teacup sweet emptyings, cinnamon and rosewater.

COMMON GINGER-BREAD.—Take a quart bowlful of flour, and rub into a teacup of sweet butter, two cups of sugar, three of molasses, teacup of cream, teaspoonful saleratus, ginger to your taste. Make it stiff batter, bake in a quick oven.

GINGER-BREAD.—Four cups of flour, three eggs, one cup of butter, two of sugar, one of cream, ginger, nutmeg, saleratus.

ARROW-ROOT CUSTARDS.—Four eggs, one dessertspoonful of arrow-root, one pint of milk sweetened, and spiced to the taste.

[THE END.]